Americans All biographies are inspiring life stories about people of all races, creeds, and nationalities who have uniquely contributed to the American way of life. Highlights from each person's story develop his contributions in his special field — whether they be in the arts, industry, human rights, education, science and medicine, or sports.

Specific abilities, character, and accomplishments are emphasized. Often despite great odds, these famous people have attained success in their fields through the good use of ability, determination, and hard work. These fast-moving stories of real people will show the way to better understanding of the ingredients necessary for personal success.

Andrew Carnegie

GIANT OF INDUSTRY

by Mary Malone

illustrated by Marvin Besunder

GARRARD PUBLISHING COMPANY
CHAMPAIGN, ILLINOIS

J
920
C

Picture credits:

Boatmen's National Bank of St. Louis: p. 58
Brown Brothers: p. 2, 75, 84, 87
Carnegie Corporation of New York: p. 54, 76, 92
Culver Pictures: p. 12, 78
New York Public Library, Picture Collection: p. 21, 36

Contents

1. The Old Home

Ten-year-old Andrew Carnegie doubled up his fists, ready to fight. He was on his way home from school in the town of Dunfermline, Scotland. It was 1845.

Some bigger boys were teasing him. "That's right, Andy," said one, ruffling the smaller boy's light hair. "England *is* larger than Scotland."

"I just don't believe it," Andrew said. His blue eyes flashed and his fair skin reddened. Suddenly he turned and ran down the street as fast as his short legs would carry him. He burst into his uncle's grocery shop on High Street.

"Uncle Lauder," he cried. "The boys at school tell me that England is larger than Scotland! It's not true, is it?"

Uncle Lauder looked down at Andrew's troubled face. "No, lad," he said. "Not really. Scotland would be larger if it were rolled out as flat as England is. But would you have the Highlands rolled flat?"

Andrew frowned. "No, Uncle Lauder."

"Nor would I," Uncle Lauder said.

Andrew felt better and went off to play with his cousin George, Uncle Lauder's son. Soon the two boys were in the middle of an exciting game of Stealing Sticks with their friends on the street. Forming sides, as in Prisoner's Base, two teams of children tried to snatch sticks from one another's well-guarded base.

Andrew and George always played together. They were very close. They called each other Dod and Naig, nicknames for George and Carnegie. The boys spent a great deal of time with George's father. They loved to hear him tell about Robert Bruce and William Wallace, who had fought to free Scotland from England, long ago.

On Sundays Uncle Lauder took the boys for long walks around Dunfermline. On one of their walks, they stopped at the Abbey Church, where Robert Bruce was buried. The high stone tower of the Abbey was a monument to Bruce.

"He was Scotland's first king," Uncle Lauder said, pointing to the huge stone letters on the tower.

"King Robert the Bruce," Andrew read, his heart beating fast with pride.

Next to the Abbey was Pittencrieff Glen. Long ago when William Wallace was being hunted by the English, he had hidden in the caves and forests of the Glen. Now it was a beautiful park. But Lord Hunt, who owned it, would not let any working people enter. The two boys peered through the entrance gates.

10

"I wish we could go in, don't you, Naig?" Dod asked.

Andrew nodded. "Someday," he vowed, "I shall see the inside of the Glen."

The walks always ended at the Carnegies' small stone cottage on Moodie Street. Andrew's brother, two-year-old Thomas, watched for them. When he saw them coming down the street, he would run to tell his mother, who soon had tea ready.

At the table one Sunday, as they drank their tea, Uncle Lauder and Andrew's parents talked about the hard times in Scotland. William Carnegie, Andrew's father, was a weaver. He worked in his own cottage making linen cloth. He was a gentle man and loved to sing as he worked, but lately his songs had seemed very sad.

"I have only one loom left now," he

said. "I used to have four. Soon the factories will take away all my work."

Mrs. Carnegie patted his hand. "Never mind, Will. If things get much worse, we'll leave Scotland!"

A shadow crossed her husband's face.

More relatives came to visit after tea. Soon it was time for Andrew to go to bed, but even as he was falling off to sleep he could hear their talk about

Andrew grew up in this house in Scotland.

"America" and "Pittsburgh." He knew that his mother's two sisters had settled with their families in America, near Pittsburgh, Pennsylvania.

Soon William Carnegie had even less weaving to do. His wife opened a small candy shop in their cottage. At night she mended shoes. She had learned this trade from her father, who was a shoemaker. Andrew helped by delivering orders for his mother and keeping accounts for the little shop.

Times were hard, but Andrew's home was always happy. Margaret and William Carnegie loved their children and treated them as though they were partners in the family.

2. To the West

William Carnegie came home one day and said sadly, "I have no more work. All orders are now going to factories."

Margaret Carnegie was silent and the boys sat quietly. Then she said, "You know we have a letter from my sister Aitken. She wants us to come to America. There is work there and room enough for everyone."

William was troubled. He did not want to leave his beloved Scotland.

"Think of our sons, Will," his wife urged. "We must go for their sakes."

At last he nodded, looking at Andrew and Tom. Andrew was twelve now, Tom, four. "Yes, it's best for the boys to begin life in a new country."

Once they had decided to leave Scotland, the Carnegies sold everything they owned. They still needed almost 100 dollars more to pay their fare. Their good friend Ella Henderson offered them the money.

Mrs. Carnegie was greatly touched by her friend's generosity. "This is your life savings, Ella!"

Mrs. Henderson nodded. "I'm glad I had it to give. Don't worry. You may pay me back after you get settled in America."

"Indeed we will," Mrs. Carnegie promised.

In Glasgow the Carnegies boarded a converted whaling schooner called the *Wiscasset*. Uncle Lauder and Dod came to see them off.

It was so hard to say good-bye! Andrew ran back and threw his arms around Uncle Lauder. "I can't leave you!" he cried.

Uncle Lauder comforted him. "We will write to each other, Naig. And maybe Dod and I will visit America someday."

Andrew was led aboard the ship by a sympathetic sailor. All four Carnegies wept as they stood on deck, waving at the relatives they were leaving behind. Slowly the *Wiscasset* moved out to sea.

After a few days of feeling miserable, Andrew began to explore the ship. His curiosity and friendliness made him a favorite of the sailors. They taught him such tricks of their trade as how to tie nautical knots and how to predict the weather. They even invited him to share their Sunday treat of plum cake.

It took 50 days for the *Wiscasset* to reach New York City. Then the Carnegies had to wait while immigration authorities arranged their trip to Pittsburgh, by way of Buffalo and the Erie Canal. In those days there was no railroad from New York City to the West.

The hurry and bustle of New York excited the Carnegies. To William Carnegie the city seemed like a human beehive. But the whole family suffered from the heat and the mosquitoes.

The last lap of their journey took the weary travelers up the Ohio River on a steamship. As they neared the dock in Pittsburgh, they saw familiar faces. "There's Aitken! And Kitty and William Hogan!" Mrs. Carnegie was laughing and crying at the same time.

Soon the newcomers were being hugged

and kissed, and everybody piled into a
wagon that would carry them to the
Carnegies' new home. It was in Allegheny
City, two miles across the river from
Pittsburgh.

The family settled on the second floor
of a tiny house on Rebecca Street, next
to widowed Aunt Aitken. She owned the
house and gave it to them rent free.

"We have a good start," Margaret
Carnegie assured her brood. With the
few things she had brought with her from
Scotland, she made their bare rooms look
like home. On the ground floor of their
house was a small loom that belonged
to Uncle Hogan, Aunt Kitty's husband.
William Carnegie started work at once,
using the loom to weave tablecloths. Little
Tom was to go to school as soon as he
was old enough. Andrew would get a job.

Andrew's mother
in later life

It was not easy for a boy to get work.
There were no laws against child labor
then, but it was a time when many grown
men were out of work and looking for
jobs. Andrew wanted to help the family.
"Uncle Hogan says I could sell knick-
knacks down by the waterfront," he said.

His mother turned to him, eyes flash-
ing. It was one of the few times in his

life Andrew saw her angry. "Never!" she declared. "I will not let you go down there to mingle with low characters, peddling cheap trinkets."

When his mother spoke in that tone of voice, Andrew knew that she meant what she said.

Soon William Carnegie was looking for a job too. Nobody in Allegheny City wanted to buy fine linen. When someone told him of a cotton mill that needed workers, he and Andrew hurried off to apply. The owner was a fellow Scot and hired both of them. The two Carnegies were delighted to be working, even though their work day lasted from six o'clock in the morning until six o'clock at night.

Andrew became a "bobbin boy," tending a machine that wound thread around the bobbins, or spools. He was paid $1.20

a week. After a few months he was offered another, harder job at $2.00 a week.
He fired the boiler that provided steam
to run the machinery in the factory. Between times, he dipped the new bobbins
in a big tub of oil. The oil treatment,
before the bobbins were painted, reduced
the friction when the thread was wound

on the metal spools. For Andrew, the worst part of his job was the smell of oil.

"No matter how hard I try, Mother," he said, "I just can't seem to wash that smell off."

His mother tried to help him by washing and ironing his work clothes every evening. Soon she had to take in washing for other people too, because William Carnegie became sick and could no longer work in the mill. He grew better slowly but was never able to do hard work again. He went back to weaving and tried selling his linens from door to door, but he was not very successful. Mrs. Carnegie took on extra work by mending shoes for the neighborhood shoemaker. It was a hard life, but through it all she was strong and cheerful.

Sometimes Andrew wished he were back

in Dunfermline, enjoying the companion-ship of Dod and Uncle Lauder. He wrote to them often. In spite of all the prob-lems the Carnegies were having, Andrew was always optimistic. "Anyone who works hard can get along in this country," he said in one letter. "The future is bright. Today, Father took out naturalization papers. Before long we will be American citizens!"

Saturday nights were Andrew's happiest times. It was then that he turned over his weekly earnings to his mother.

"You're doing a man's job, Andrew," she said. "I'm proud of you!"

Those words made up to Andrew for all his hard work.

3. Telegraph Boy

Andrew soon had friends on Rebecca Street. His quick wit and cheerful disposition made him popular with the other boys. Although he worked six days a week, he and his friends had good times on Sundays. When the weather was good, they hiked to the woods. In winter they went skating on the frozen Allegheny River, then gathered hungrily in Mrs. Carnegie's kitchen. She baked sweet biscuits she called scones for the boys and told them stories of Scottish history.

Andrew loved learning and wished he could have more education. When he heard about a night school in Pittsburgh where he could study bookkeeping, he urged some of his friends to go with him. Three of them did. Every night that winter, except on Saturdays and Sundays, they all trudged to Pittsburgh and back. This was Andrew's only schooling in the United States.

He worked as a bobbin boy for almost a year. Then one evening he returned home to find his Uncle Hogan there. "Good news, Andrew! They need a messenger boy at the telegraph office in Pittsburgh."

Andrew's heart leaped. This was his chance. "I'm going to apply for the job," he told his parents. His father was not encouraging. He thought that the telegraph office would probably want an older boy for such a responsible job.

"Let me try, Father." Andrew begged.

William Carnegie nodded. "All right, lad. I'll go with you when you apply."

The next morning, on the way to the telegraph office, Andrew said, "Father, I want to get this job myself. Please wait outside for me."

Mr. Carnegie agreed, and Andrew went into the office by himself. Politely, he explained his purpose. The manager was impressed. "How old are you?" he asked.

"Fourteen," Andrew replied. "I know I'm small, but just give me a chance, Mr. Brooks."

"When can you go to work?"

"Right now!"

"That's fine," Mr. Brooks said. Then he turned to another boy who had been watching them. "Davy, come and meet our new messenger."

28

"He's pretty small," Davy mumbled.

"Just you wait," Andrew told the boy good-naturedly. He quickly found out what his duties were to be. Then he ran out to his father with the good news.

Before long Andrew knew the names of all the streets in Pittsburgh. Soon, too, he knew by sight the important men in the city, those who received many messages. He saved time by delivering telegrams to them right on the street.

"There's Colonel Anderson," Davy told Andrew one day.

"Why, he's the man who's opened his own library to working boys," Andrew exclaimed. "I'd like to read those books!"

"We're not 'working boys,'" Davy said.

"We are," insisted Andrew. "You don't have to work with your hands to be a working boy. As soon as I have a chance,

I'm going to ask Colonel Anderson if we can read his books."

Not long afterward he had to deliver a telegram to Colonel Anderson. "Sir," he burst out, "messenger boys and office boys are working boys too! We'd like to use your library."

Colonel Anderson looked seriously at Andrew. Then he gave a nod and said, "Young man, you and your friends may come any Saturday afternoon."

After that Andrew never stopped reading. He always carried a book in his pocket and used every spare moment to read. He had to work and could no longer go to school, but he educated himself in history, literature, and economics.

The telegraph business grew, and more messenger boys were needed. Andrew recommended two of his neighborhood chums. They were hired and joined Andrew and Davy, who by this time had become close friends. The four boys had some good times together, with Andrew as the leader. One day Andrew settled a quarrel over the extra dimes messengers received for delivering telegrams outside the city limits. "We'll pool the dimes," he decided, "and divide the money evenly at the end of the week."

"All right, Andy," Davy agreed. "You be treasurer."

There were no more arguments after that.

Andrew always remembered the first time he delivered a telegram to the Pittsburgh Theater. It was winter, and he was glad to get in out of the cold. He glanced at the stage and his attention was caught. An eerie scene was being enacted. Flashes of lightning revealed three witches dancing round a fire. Thunder crashed and rolled and then the witches began to speak. The words were solemn, yet strangely beautiful. Andrew shivered, but not from the cold.

"What play is that?" he asked.

"*Macbeth*, by Shakespeare," an usher told him.

"I must see more!" Andrew exclaimed.

"The peanut gallery is open," said the usher carelessly. "Only fifteen cents."

Andrew nodded. "I'll come back."

After that he spent almost every Saturday night in the gallery. In addition, he caught glimpses of the plays and concerts whenever he delivered a telegram to the theater. He heard Jenny Lind, the famous Swedish singer, and was thrilled by Wagner's musical drama *Lohengrin*, but his greatest love was for Shakespeare. He borrowed a book of Shakespeare's plays and memorized long passages. All his life Andrew took pleasure in quoting Shakespeare.

Andrew liked his job. He arrived before anyone else and swept out the office.

He sharpened pencils and studied the telegraph machine. One morning when he was alone in the office, the telegraph machine began to click with the sound that meant an urgent message was waiting. Andrew decided to take it. He knew how because he had watched and listened as the operators worked. "Go ahead," he signaled. Then he turned the key that started the dots and dashes coming over

Sixteen-year-old Andrew, shown here with his brother Tom, earned a man's salary.

the wire. Already, Andrew had learned the Morse alphabet, so he was able to decode the message. He delivered it, and afterward told the manager. Mr. Brooks gave him only a cool nod.

"You had a nerve, Andy," the other boys said.

When the next payday came, the boys

lined up as usual for their salaries. Andrew was first in line. But this time Mr. Brooks passed him by and paid the next boy. Andrew's heart sank as he watched each boy get his pay and leave. He was sure he was going to be fired. Finally he was the only one left.

Then Mr. Brooks turned to him and smiled. "Your pay is raised to $13.50 a month, Andy. You're worth more than the other boys."

Andrew stammered his thanks as Mr. Brooks shook hands with him. He couldn't wait to tell his parents. When they heard the happy report, the Carnegies were prouder than ever of their son. "It's no more than you deserved, Andrew," his mother said.

Now Andrew substituted for the regular operators when they were sick. At sixteen, he became a full-time operator, earning $25 a month, a man's salary. Life became easier for his family. The Carnegies bought a small house of their own and some new furniture. Best of all, they sent Ella Henderson her money. They had been saving in order to repay her. At last they had enough.

"Hooray, Mother, we're out of debt!" Andrew exclaimed. "Let's have a celebration on Saturday night!"

The relatives were invited, and they all talked and sang far into the night. Life in America seemed full of promise to the Carnegies.

4. Railroad Man

Andrew was a telegraph operator for a year. Then in 1852 the Pennsylvania Railroad came to Pittsburgh. The job of cutting a railway line through the mountains to join Pittsburgh with Philadelphia had just been completed.

Mr. Thomas Scott, superintendent of the railroad's western division, was a frequent visitor to the telegraph office. He liked Andrew and offered the young man a job on the railroad.

Andrew had decided he was going to the top wherever he might work. The Pennsylvania Railroad was a big, growing company. It promised a good chance for advancement. So Andrew left the telegraph office and went to work for the railroad as a telegraph operator and clerk to Mr. Scott. One of his first duties was to go to Altoona, more than 100 miles away, for the monthly payroll.

Andrew felt proud and important to be handling the payroll. He would fasten it to his belt and ride back to Pittsburgh in the cab of the train with the engineer. The ride was rough, with much shaking and jolting. Rails were made of wood in those days and were held up by stone blocks.

One day he was halfway home before he reached for the payroll to check on

its safety. He was horrified to find it was gone. "Stop!" he shouted. "I've lost the payroll!" This was dreadful. What would Mr. Scott think of him?

The train jerked to a stop. "Can you back up?" Andrew asked the engineer.

"I can, Andy," the engineer replied. "My wages are in that payroll too. Keep an eye out below." He backed the train while Andrew leaned out, watching the ground.

Andrew was almost ready to give up hope when he spotted the bag at the edge of a stream. He called to the engineer, jumped out, and snatched the payroll from the ground. A few more feet and the bag would have been in the water. Andrew held it tightly all the way back to Pittsburgh. Never again, he vowed, would he forget his responsibility.

This experience didn't stop him from taking risks, however. One day when Mr. Scott was late getting to the office, the report of an accident came over the telegraph wire. A freight car had overturned and was blocking the track. Trains could not travel in either direction. The freight car had to be moved—quickly. Andrew wired orders in Mr. Scott's name.

Mr. Scott hurried back to the office when he heard the news of the accident.

43

"It's all taken care of, Mr. Scott," Andrew said. Then he explained.

Mr. Scott looked surprised, but he said nothing. From then on, however, he often allowed Andrew to give the train orders.

Shortly afterward Mr. Scott became chief superintendent of the railroad. He appointed Andrew as his secretary, at a higher salary. Andrew's new job took him back and forth to Altoona. On one trip a man found out where Andrew was sitting and came to sit beside him. "I understand you are connected with the Pennsylvania Railroad," he said. Then he opened his bag and took out a small-scale railroad car. "This is something I have invented. It's a sleeping car."

Andrew examined the invention with growing interest. The railroads were expanding. Soon they would need special

cars with berths so that passengers could
sleep when they traveled at night. "I'll
speak to the superintendent," he promised
the inventor. When he did, he was so
convincing that Mr. Scott ordered sleeping cars for the Pennsylvania Railroad.
Even before the sleeping cars became a
success, Andrew had faith in them. He
borrowed money from a bank in order

to buy a share in the business. It was his first investment.

Mr. Scott was promoted to the vice-presidency of the railroad, with his office in Philadelphia. As a result of his own promotion, he gave Andrew a big boost up the ladder of success. "Do you think you could manage the Pennsylvania's Pittsburgh division, Andy?" he asked.

Could he? Andrew was sure he could manage anything, even this big job. But he said modestly, "Yes, I think I can, Mr. Scott."

Life was certainly improving for the Carnegies. Then tragedy struck. William Carnegie died after years of poor health. Andrew was sad to think he had not been able to give his father a comfortable life soon enough. He tried to make up for it with his mother. As soon as he could, he bought a country house away from the smoke and grime of the city, in Homewood, outside of Pittsburgh. He hired servants to do the hardest work. Mrs. Carnegie could ride in her carriage and visit her friends and relatives whenever she wished. Tom finished school and became Andrew's clerk. He was steady and reliable, a great help to his quicker, livelier brother.

About this time Andrew began to enjoy parties and dances. There he made new friends, some of them young ladies. He began to pay more attention to his appearance and his way of speaking. He looked and acted like a gentleman, but he never lost his simple, friendly air.

5. Civil War Work

Slavery was something Andrew could never explain in his letters to Dod and Uncle Lauder. He himself was an abolitionist; the abolitionists believed slavery should be done away with. Andrew even wrote letters to the newspapers stating his belief that slavery should be abolished. Abraham Lincoln became one of his heroes, just as Bruce and Wallace had been in his childhood. He was glad when Lincoln was elected President in 1860.

But he watched anxiously as the Southern states began to leave the Union, and form their own government, called the Confederacy.

The situation grew worse when the Confederate soldiers seized some United States forts. Then they fired on Fort Sumter in South Carolina when it would not surrender to them. This action started the Civil War.

Andrew Carnegie decided to do whatever he could to help the Union. "This country has been good to me," he said.

Mr. Scott was appointed Assistant Secretary of War, in charge of railroads and telegraphs for the Army. He asked Andrew to help him.

The war was going badly for the Union. The Confederates surged into Maryland, where they pulled up the railroad tracks and tore down the telegraph lines. Union troops could not get to Washington or reach the front in Virginia, where fighting had begun. The Secretary of War was worried. Andrew was summoned and given his orders. "Find another route for the trains to get through!"

Andrew knew about an old branch line below Baltimore that might be repaired. But he had to hurry. The Capitol—the President himself—was in danger of being captured by Confederate troops if help did not get to Washington soon. Andrew and his men worked day and night. At last the tracks were clear and Andrew rode in the first train to go through. During the trip he saw a telegraph line down and jumped off to fix it. As he pulled out the stake holding the wire to the ground, the wire sprang up and hit

him in the face. Blood spurted from a deep cut on his cheek. Covering it with his handkerchief, Andrew went on to Washington. He joked about the cut, saying, "I'm glad to shed blood for my country."

His war work had only begun. His next job was to move troops across the Potomac River into Virginia. The bridge had been destroyed, and Andrew had to supervise the building of a new one. Later Andrew was stationed in Alexandria, Virginia, to keep the telegraph lines to the battle front open. He watched the Union soldiers march through Alexandria, laughing and singing. They declared they would whip the Southern army and end the war in a few weeks. "On to Richmond!" they shouted. Richmond was the capital of the Confederacy.

But the Confederate soldiers were waiting at Bull Run. In a fierce battle there, the Union forces were beaten. They came pouring back to Alexandria in disorderly retreat. Andrew rushed trains and engines up to the battle front to remove the dead and wounded.

It was his first sight of war's brutality, and what he saw sickened him. For the rest of his life, he hated war. "There *must* be a better way to settle differences," he thought.

The Civil War dragged on. Andrew organized the Army's transportation and communication systems. When the Union side at last began to win, both Mr. Scott and Andrew were called back by the Pennsylvania Railroad. Important tasks awaited them. Arms and ammunition had to be shipped to the front; troops had to

Andrew had earned the first of his fortune when he was still a very young man.

be moved. Andrew worked so hard he became ill and was given time off to get better.

He decided to return to Scotland for a visit. His mother went with him. While she went about visiting her many relatives in Dunfermline, Andrew stayed with

Dod and Uncle Lauder. The three of them never stopped talking. At twenty-six, Andrew delighted in being "Naig" again.

The cool, clean air of Scotland made him feel so much better that he said he'd like to spend every summer there. "I'll be back," he promised when he and his mother left for the United States.

Leaving Scotland was not the sad occasion it had been fourteen years before. Now Andrew looked forward with confidence to his future in America.

6. Iron and Steel

Andrew returned to his job rested and strong. He and Tom began to look for ways to improve the railroad.

One day they stood at the window of their office watching a work gang repairing the tracks.

"We lose too much time in repairing wooden rails," Andrew said.

Tom nodded. "Bridges, too."

Suddenly Andrew snapped his fingers. "I remember seeing a little iron bridge near Altoona! Why can't *we* build iron bridges instead of wooden ones? Iron bridges won't burn down or be washed away so easily in a flood."

"Let's try," Tom suggested. "First we'll find the man in Altoona who built the iron bridge."

When people heard of the Carnegies' plan, some said that iron couldn't support wide spans across a river or hold up heavy trains.

Andrew told them, "If we can't build a safe bridge, we won't build any."

This became his policy in all his work. Only the best quality was good enough for a Carnegie product.

The iron bridges were successful. Then Andrew tried iron rails instead of the wooden ones that the railroads had been using for years. These, too, were a big improvement. Next, with his partners,

Carnegie's iron rails and bridges made the westward growth of the railroads possible.

Andrew built iron mills to produce the materials for rails and bridges. His business was booming. He began to invest some of his money in oil fields, and in insurance companies. Soon he was making so much money from his own companies that he decided to leave the Pennsylvania Railroad. He was only thirty years old, but from that time on he never worked

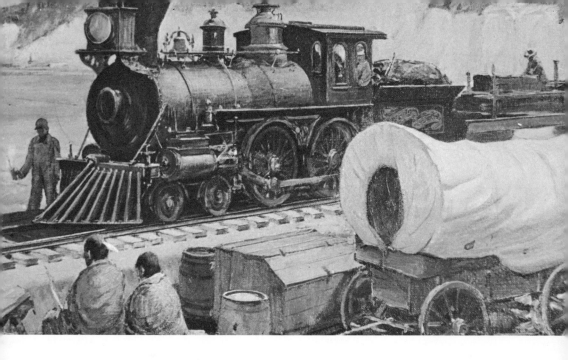

for a salary from others. Young as he was, he could afford to be his own boss.

The railroads became Carnegie's best customers. They were growing bigger and bigger, crisscrossing the country from east to west and from west to east. More and more rails and bridges were needed. More iron was needed for the bridges and rails. More sleeping cars were being used—and more locomotives. Soon Andrew started another company to make locomotives. In all of the Carnegie companies, he was the chief partner.

It was time now, he decided, to move to New York City, the business capital of the country. He would be close to other business concerns and better able to sell the Carnegie products. His mother moved with him, and they lived in a large apartment in one of New York's best hotels. Tom remained in Pittsburgh as business manager of the Carnegie companies and moved into the house at Homewood with his new wife.

Andrew's business methods seemed daring to Tom and to some of the other partners. Andrew was always shrewd and practical, however. If he learned about another company that made a product similar to his, he did not waste time fighting but got the company to join him.

By this time he owned the original sleeping car business. But a man named George Pullman was making sleeping cars, too, and selling them to railroads in the West. He and Andrew both wanted to sell their cars to the big Union Pacific Railroad. Andrew went directly to Mr. Pullman and said, "Let's stop making fools of ourselves."

Surprised, Mr. Pullman asked Andrew, "What do you mean?"

Andrew smiled. "We are now working against each other. The railroads will beat us down. If we unite and become one company, we'll both move ahead."

Mr. Pullman frowned. "What would you call the company?"

"Why, the Pullman Palace Car Company," Andrew replied promptly.

Mr. Pullman relaxed. The name pleased

him. Besides, he knew that Carnegie was right. "I'll join you," he said. Together, they won a big contract from the Union Pacific.

Always, Carnegie searched restlessly for new ways to do things. He heard about a process used in England that made iron into steel. He went over to see how it was done and to meet the man who had invented it, Henry Bessemer. He saw a furnace where air was forced through crude iron, burning out carbon and other impurities in the iron. What was left was steel—a stronger, tougher metal.

Andrew returned home, excited by what he had seen. "We should start making steel at once," he told Tom and the other partners. "Just think what this means! Steel will replace iron just as iron re-placed wood. We have no time to lose!"

The others were not interested. One of the partners said, "A few companies tried to use this Bessemer process and failed."

Tom nodded. "We've been successful because we worked hard and used sensible methods," he said. "Why risk what we've built up for this new method we're not sure of?"

Andrew laughed. "All right. I'll start a new company, with new partners!"

"This is no time to build, Andy," one of the partners warned. "We're going through a depression."

Andrew turned to him quickly. "It's the best time to build," he said. "I can do it more cheaply now. Then I'll be ready to take orders when prosperity returns."

While the others shook their heads and called him reckless, he continued, "I have the cash to construct the first steel works in America. And I'm going to do it!"

Carnegie had an unshakable faith in the future growth of America. He sold most of his stock in his other companies and put the money into a new steel plant. Then he went out and persuaded railroads to give him orders. He knew his customers and he gave them a fair price. With the new Bessemer process, Carnegie made steel the outstanding industry of Pittsburgh. His steel mills worked day and night, their great blast furnaces shooting flames high into the sky.

One of the reasons for Carnegie's success was his judgment of men. He picked good men to work for him. One of these was Captain Bill Jones. Andrew chose Bill Jones to manage the Edgar Thomson Steel Company. Then Carnegie bought the

Homestead Mills. He now owned the largest steel complex in the world, with 30,000 workers. Big, brawny Bill Jones was a fighter as well as a worker. He knew the steel business and he was enthusiastic about the new Bessemer process. Under his leadership the men in the Edgar Thomson Steel Company became experts at making steel.

"I worked with Bill Jones!" was the proud

boast of many Pittsburgh steel workers.

Carnegie thought so highly of Bill that he offered him a partnership in the company.

Bill looked down at the short, stocky little Scotsman. Then he shook his head. "No, thanks, Boss. I have enough to do looking after the mill."

Carnegie knew Bill would miss the men if he had to work in an office. "What would you like, then?" he asked, smiling.

Bill laughed. "Just pay me a whopping big salary if you think I'm worth it."

Without any hesitation, Carnegie agreed. "It's yours. From now on, Bill, you'll get the same salary as the President of the United States."

When his partners complained, Carnegie only said, "Where would you find another Bill Jones?"

One day in 1889 Bill himself shut down the steel mills. "Johnstown is flooded!" Bill shouted to his workers. "They need our help!"

After many days of heavy rain, Lake Conemaugh, in the Allegheny Mountains above the town of Johnstown, had over-flowed. The old earthwork dam, which was supposed to hold back the lake waters from the valley below, gave way. The water roared down on Johnstown, smashing everything in its path. Thousands of people were drowned in one of the worst disasters in American history.

Bill Jones and his men piled into freight cars and rode the 70 miles from Pittsburgh to Johnstown. They all worked for days, helping the homeless and bewildered people there.

Later that year the Edgar Thomson Works was the scene of a terrible accident. One of the furnaces exploded, killing six men who were near it. Bill Jones was one of them.

Some time later when Andrew Carnegie built his home in New York, he placed a big picture of Bill Jones on the wall. To everyone who saw it hanging there, he said, *"He* was the greatest steel maker of them all."

7. A Castle in Scotland

Andrew Carnegie was a millionaire by the time he was forty. He knew now that just making a fortune would not satisfy him. He began to think of using money to help others. He was encouraged in these ideas by many of his friends, who were well-known writers and thinkers.

Travel helped him to understand people better. It also gave him much-needed vacations from the business of steel-making. "Travel is good medicine, Tom," he told his brother. "I wish you would come with me." But Tom never wanted to leave the business.

Two friends went with Andrew on a walking tour through Europe. A few years later, they sailed around the world. Then Andrew took his mother and a party of friends on his famous "coaching trip." When they landed in England, Andrew hired a "coach and four," a carriage pulled by four horses, to take his party to Inverness, Scotland. For seven weeks they drove through the lovely summer countryside, staying at inns overnight, stopping often along the way just to pick flowers or go wading in a brook. Andrew's only regret was that Louise Whitfield had not consented to come along. She was a charming young woman he had met in New York. Someday he would ask her to marry him.

The coaching party stopped one day in Dunfermline, and Andrew dedicated the public library he had given the town. Everyone turned out to see him. The streets were decorated with flowers and flags. The band played *The Star-Spangled Banner*. Even the Abbey bells were ringing for him.

This trip gave Andrew material for his first book, *An American Four-in-hand in Britain*. It was published in 1883 and became quite popular, so he wrote several others—about his travels and his ideas on government and wealth.

In the summer of 1886 Andrew went with his mother to their cottage at Cresson, in the Allegheny Mountains. Mrs. Carnegie was seventy-six now and growing feeble. Andrew himself did not feel well, but he expected the mountain air

of Cresson to cure him. Instead, he grew worse and had to go to bed. When the doctor came, he found that Andrew had typhoid fever.

For six weeks Andrew was very sick. He did not know anything that was going on. Tom came to see him. Shortly after he went back to Pittsburgh, Tom was stricken with pneumonia and died. Then Mrs. Carnegie became critically ill. She died soon after Tom. Andrew was not told about the deaths of his mother and brother until he was better, many weeks later. He went back to New York, sad and lonely.

Louise Whitfield was the first to call on him. Now, he and she both knew they did not want to be separated again. They were married in April and went to Scotland on their wedding trip. Andrew's

Andrew's wife, Louise, as she might have dressed for a ball

relatives there were charmed by his bride. "We couldn't have picked a better wife for Andrew," they said.

When the Carnegies' daughter was born, Louise said to Andrew, "We'll name her Margaret, after your mother."

Louise loved Scotland as much as her husband did. She wanted to spend every summer there, so Andrew looked for a place to buy. He found Skibo, an old castle overlooking the sea. The country around it was beautiful, with lakes and woods, and near the castle was a sandy beach where little Margaret could play. Andrew put in electricity and plumbing and improved the villages surrounding his estate, giving each one a school and a library. The village people called him

Skibo, a castle home for three Carnegies

"Laird of Skibo." All Scotland was proud of him.

The Carnegies entertained many friends at Skibo—famous people as well as their own special friends, whom they called "old shoes." Even the King of England paid them a surprise visit, arriving when Andrew was taking a nap. The King especially liked the two flags flying together over the house—the Union Jack and the Stars and Stripes. "You've done a great deal to improve relations between Britain and America, Carnegie," he said.

In New York the Carnegies built their town house on Fifth Avenue across from Central Park. In it Andrew had the things he liked best—books, music, and an art gallery.

America's growth seemed boundless, and steel was its basic product. So Andrew

Carnegie kept making more and more money. He was incredibly wealthy. But he and his family lived simply, without wasting money on their own pleasures. Sometimes Andrew said jokingly, "I'm going to make sure I die poor."

He was serious, however, about the idea of giving his fortune away. He even wrote about his plan in a book he called *The Gospel of Wealth*.

The Carnegies' New York town house

8. The Richest Man in the World

Andrew Carnegie was in Scotland in July 1892 when trouble started in Homestead. Henry Frick was now in charge of the mill. Frick was a good manager, and under his leadership profits doubled. Andrew could spend more time doing the things he liked—traveling, writing, and public speaking. With Frick, business profits came first. He seemed cold and aloof to the workers. His relations with them grew worse, and the men said they would strike for higher wages. Frick's answer was to close the mill.

Frick hired new workers to take the places of those on strike and brought in private policemen. This made the Homestead people very angry, and they began to riot in the streets. Outsiders came and added to the violence. The town was a scene of terror. The Governor of Pennsylvania ordered soldiers of the National Guard to restore order in Homestead.

Before the fighting was stopped, 10 men were killed and 60 were wounded. Henry Frick was shot as he sat in his office. Fortunately, he recovered. His attacker was caught and later sent to prison.

All this was terrible news for Andrew Carnegie. He was especially upset over the bloodshed. "The workers and I could

have agreed," he said. "I have always been on their side." It was true that the workers trusted Andrew Carnegie, whom they called "the little boss." The Homestead trouble might not have happened if he had been there, but still he had to take the blame. He and Henry Frick were never on good terms after that, and Andrew finally bought out Frick's share in the Carnegie companies.

Andrew sent word to his partners to appoint Charles Schwab as manager of Homestead, in Mr. Frick's place. "Smiling Charlie" was Schwab's nickname. He had started out as a pile driver under Captain Bill Jones, and worked his way up to become chief engineer and then manager of the Edgar Thompson Works. Carnegie liked Charlie Schwab because the young man was bright and eager to succeed.

He got along well with his men. Before long, he became Carnegie's most trusted partner.

Andrew Carnegie was sixty-five now. Although he was active and alert, he felt it was time to retire. He decided to sell his steel business. His partners agreed.

"There's only one man who can pay our price," Andrew told Charlie Schwab. "That's J.P. Morgan, the richest banker in the country."

Charlie Schwab was sent to talk with Morgan. Schwab was a good salesman. At last the banker said, "Well, if Andy wants to sell, I'll buy. What price is he asking?"

Schwab was ready. "The price is $300,000,000."

Without blinking an eyelash, Morgan nodded. "I'll take it."

After J.P. Morgan bought the Carnegie Steel Company, it became known as the United States Steel Corporation.

Later Morgan and Carnegie met on a ship going to Europe. They sat in their deck chairs and talked for a while. Then J.P. Morgan turned to his companion and said, "Carnegie, if you had asked a hundred million more, I would have paid it."

Carnegie smiled. "That doesn't bother me at all." He didn't add what everyone knew—that he was already the wealthiest man in the world.

"The wealthiest man in the world" at his desk after the sale of his steel business

9. A Promise Kept

Andrew Carnegie was ready now for a new kind of business—giving money away. But he was not satisfied just to give money to charity. "I want my money used to wipe out evils and do away with ignorance," he said.

As his first big step in giving away money, he set aside several million dollars in pensions for his former mill workers. Then he began giving money for libraries.

He wanted to make good books available to everyone. He could still remember how important books were to him when he was a "working boy." He offered cities money to build free libraries if they would provide the sites and take care of the buildings. He was delighted when many cities responded. "I am now giving away libraries at the rate of two or three a day," he announced.

Carnegie donating a library at a ceremony

More than 2,000 free libraries all over the world were built with Carnegie millions. "Let there be light" was carved over the doors of many of them. Many were named for Andrew, but he was just as pleased to have them called "Free Public Libraries."

He gave cities money for museums and concert halls too. One of these was Carnegie Hall in New York City. He also established the Carnegie Institution in Washington, D.C., for scientific study. Through this institution Mount Wilson Observatory, with its great telescope to explore the heavens, was built in California.

Andrew also took great delight in helping colleges, especially small, struggling ones that educated the children of poor people. He gave scholarships and new buildings to some, special funds to others.

Among the many he helped were two for the education of Negroes—Hampton Institute and Tuskegee Institute. Then, because Andrew thought young people should be trained for trades and homemaking as well as for the professions, he built Carnegie Institute of Technology in Pittsburgh.

One day a secretary handed him a newspaper. "That man was a hero," the secretary said, pointing to an article on the front page.

Andrew read the article. It told about a coal miner who died trying to save other men trapped in a cave-in. Andrew was touched by the story. He said, "I'd like to reward deeds like this."

The bravery of an unknown coal miner inspired Carnegie's "Hero Fund," for heroic deeds in peace time. People all over the world who saved the lives of others were given medals and awards. If they lost their own lives, pensions were given to their families. The fund was one of Andrew's favorite charities.

Carnegie tried to find all the people who had helped him in his early years. He wanted to help them now. Often, if they had died, he gave pensions to their families. He also gave pensions to many others—retired college professors, writers, and poets. He gave allowances to many deserving people who had no means of their own. One of them was Helen Keller, whose courage in overcoming deafness and blindness made her famous. Thousands of persons were included in Carnegie's "pension list." When Mark Twain, the writer, who was a good friend of Andrew Carnegie's, heard about the pensions, he declared, "I'm going to call you *Saint Andrew.*"

One day, in a letter from Dod, Andrew read, "Naig, Pittencrieff Glen is for sale at last." At once Andrew cabled back, "Buy it!" He gave the Glen to Dunfermline, asking only that the gates be always open. The people of Dunfermline were so grateful they called Andrew Carnegie "Laird of Pittencrieff."

"That's the grandest title on earth," he declared. "Better than King of England."

Many of his gifts were for the betterment of the entire world. The greatest of these, he thought, was the Endowment for International Peace. Hoping to live long enough to see the end of war, Carnegie gave millions of dollars to this fund to educate people in the ways of peace. He built the Peace Palace at The

Carnegie, the "Laird of Pittencrieff," with his collie dog in Scotland

Hague in Holland and worked hard to make his dream of a world without war come true. He even went to visit the German Kaiser and tried to get him to keep the peace. Carnegie thought he had succeeded. Then in 1914, when Andrew was seventy-nine, World War I started. He was heartbroken to see that his peace efforts had failed.

For ten years, Andrew Carnegie gave away money—more than $300,000,000. He received thousands of requests for help, and he tried to grant them all. He even paid off the mortgage on an old lady's home because she reminded him of his mother.

Still his wealth kept growing faster than he could spend it. At this rate, his wife would have a heavy burden of responsibility after his death. So he told

Louise, "I'll leave enough for you and Margaret to take care of all your needs. The rest I'll turn over to a corporation that will continue to distribute my money." Louise was happy with this arrangement. The Carnegie Corporation, which Andrew formed, has carried on his charities ever since, and Carnegie money is still being given to worthy causes.

Now Andrew had time to enjoy his remaining years. He played golf with his friends and took daily walks around Central Park. Newspaper reporters followed the bouncy little man with the white hair and the white beard wherever he went. They wanted to know his opinion on everything. He told them he felt that now he had paid back the debt he owed the world. "I've had more than my share of life's blessings," he said.

In 1919 Andrew Carnegie was eighty-four. His strength was slowly failing, but he was able to enjoy two family celebrations that year. First his daughter was married, and he danced briefly at her wedding. Then Dod came from Scotland to visit—for the last time. The two old men spent many hours talking about their long ago childhood in Dunfermline. Andrew died a few months later.

Praise for Andrew Carnegie poured in from the great and famous of the world. They called him "Steel King" and "Nation Builder." His closest friends remembered what Andrew himself had said, years before. "My purpose in life is to do as much good as I can."